HOW TO DRAW™
LONDON

Mark Bergin

SALARIYA

Published in Great Britain in MMXIV by
Book House, an imprint of
The Salariya Book Company Ltd
25 Marlborough Place, Brighton BN1 1UB

1 3 5 7 9 8 6 4 2

Author: **Mark Bergin** was born in Hastings in 1961. He
studied at Eastbourne College of Art and has specialised in
historical reconstructions as well as aviation and maritime
subjects since 1983. He lives in Bexhill-on-Sea with his
wife and three children.

Editor: Victoria England

PB ISBN: 978-1-909645-12-7

A CIP catalogue record for this
book is available from the
British Library.

Printed and bound in China.
Printed on paper from
sustainable sources.

**WARNING: Fixatives should be used
only under adult supervision.**

Visit our websites to read
interactive **free** web books, stay up
to date with new releases, catch
up with us on the
Book House Blog, view our
electronic catalogue and more!

www.salariya.com
Free electronic versions of four of
our *You Wouldn't Want to Be* titles

www.book-house.co.uk
Online catalogue
Information books
and graphic novels

www.scribobooks.com
Fiction books

www.scribblersbooks.com
Books for babies, toddlers and
pre-school children

**www.flickr.com/photos/
salariyabookhouse**
View our photostream with sneak
previews of forthcoming titles

Join the conversation on Facebook
and Twitter by visiting
www.salariya.com

Visit our YouTube channel to see
Mark Bergin doing step-by-step
illustrations:
**www.youtube.com/user/
theSalariya**

Visit
www.salariya.com
for our online catalogue and
free interactive web books.

PAPER FROM
SUSTAINABLE
FORESTS

Contents

Making a start

Learning to draw is about looking and seeing. Keep practising and get to know your subject. Use a sketchbook to make quick drawings. Start by doodling, and experiment with shapes and patterns. There are many ways to draw, and this book shows only some of them. Visit art galleries, look at artists' drawings, see how friends draw, but above all, find your own way.

Try using basic shapes and construction lines to better understand forms and proportions.

Black cab

Buckingham Palace

Try keeping a sketchbook handy at all times. Practise spending ten minutes or so just getting the essence of the object down.

Millennium Footbridge

Nelson's Column

London Eye

Practice makes perfect. If your
first attempt doesn't look right,
don't be afraid to start again.

The 'Gherkin'

Tower Bridge

Drawing materials

Try using different types of drawing paper and materials. Experiment with charcoal, wax crayons and pastels. All pens, from felt—tips to ballpoints, will make interesting marks — you could also try drawing with pen and ink on wet paper.

Nelson's Column: Ink silhouette

Silhouette is a style of drawing that shows only a solid black shape, like a shadow.

Eros in Piccadilly Circus: Colour pastel

Pastels are incredibly soft and come in a wide range of colours.

The Shard: Felt—tip pen

Life Guard: Ink pen

Lines drawn in **ink** cannot be erased, so keep your ink drawings sketchy and less rigid. Don't worry about mistakes, as these lines can be lost in the drawing as it develops.

Charcoal is another very soft medium. It can be used for big, bold drawings. Ask an adult to spray your charcoal drawings with fixative to prevent smudging.

St Paul's Cathedral: Pencil

Hard **pencils** are greyer and soft pencils are blacker. Hard pencils are usually graded from 6H (the hardest) through 5H, 4H, 3H and 2H to H.

Soft pencils are graded from B, 2B, 3B, 4B and 5B up to 6B (the softest). HB is betweeen H and B.

Perspective

If you look at any object from different viewpoints, you will see that the parts that are closest to you look larger, and the parts that are further away look smaller. Perspective drawing uses this effect to create a feeling of depth. It is a way of suggesting three dimensions even though the drawing surface is really flat.

Placing the viewpoint at ground level makes the guard loom above us as if we are looking up at him.

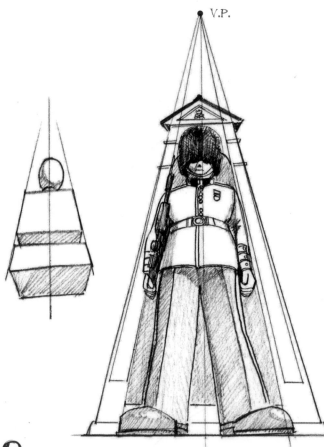

● V.P.

A single vanishing point below ground level, as with this policeman, gives the impression that we are looking down on him from above.

V.P.

The vanishing point (V.P.) is the place in a perspective drawing where parallel lines appear to meet. Simple **one—point perspective** uses only one V.P.

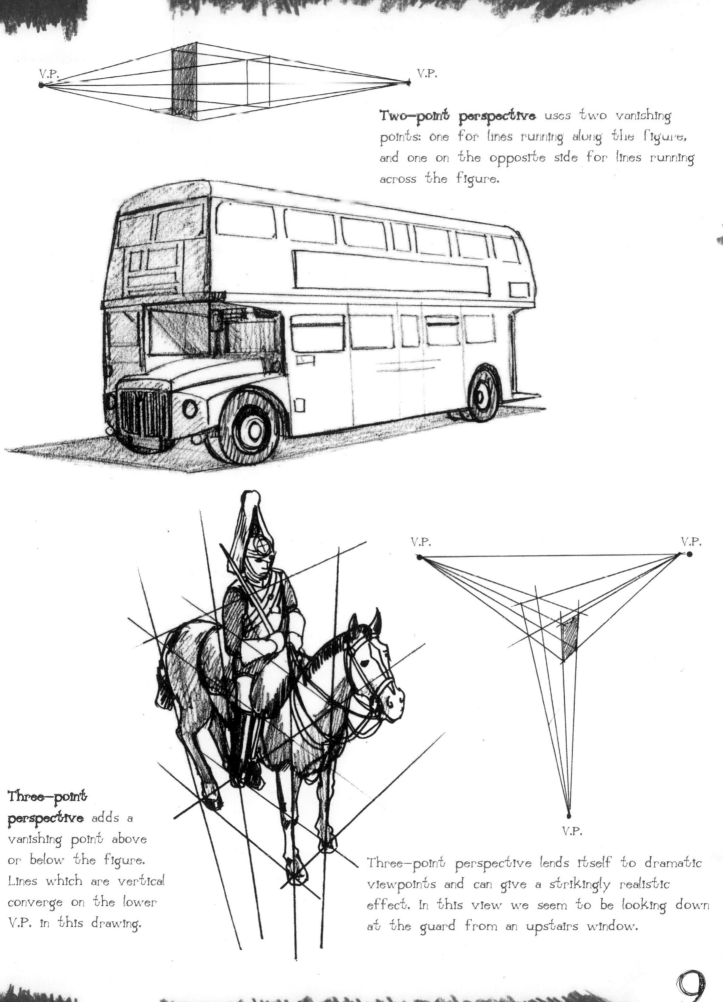

Two-point perspective uses two vanishing points: one for lines running along the figure, and one on the opposite side for lines running across the figure.

Three-point perspective adds a vanishing point above or below the figure. Lines which are vertical converge on the lower V.P. in this drawing.

Three-point perspective lends itself to dramatic viewpoints and can give a strikingly realistic effect. In this view we seem to be looking down at the guard from an upstairs window.

Using photos

Drawing from photographs is a good way to practise drawing a location — it's useful if you don't have time, or it's raining! Drawing from photographs can also help improve your eye for detail.

Tower of London

Make a tracing of your photograph and draw a grid of squares on it.

Now take a piece of drawing paper of the same proportions and draw an empty grid on it. You can enlarge or reduce your drawing by changing the size of the squares. You can now copy the shapes from each square of the tracing to the drawing paper, using the grid to guide you.

10

Light source

To make your drawing look three—dimensional, decide which side the light is coming from, and put in areas of shadow where the light does not reach.

Sketch in an overall tone and add surrounding textures to create interest and a sense of movement. Pay attention to the position of your drawing on the paper. This is called composition.

11

On the street

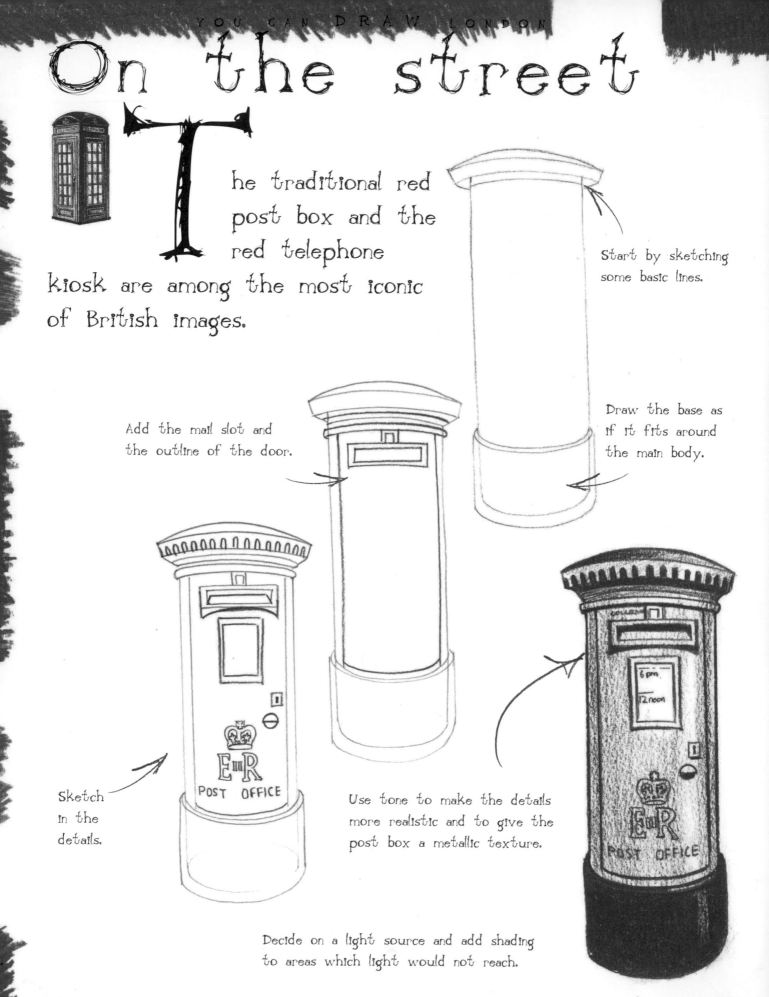

The traditional red post box and the red telephone kiosk are among the most iconic of British images.

Start by sketching some basic lines.

Draw the base as if it fits around the main body.

Add the mail slot and the outline of the door.

Sketch in the details.

6 pm
12 noon

ER
POST OFFICE

Use tone to make the details more realistic and to give the post box a metallic texture.

Decide on a light source and add shading to areas which light would not reach.

Draw three lines to make the edges of your phone box. Add a dome shape for the roof.

Sketch in lines for the roof detail, sign and door frames.

Add the decorative details, window panels and door handle.

Shade the telephone box to look shiny and add the lettering detail. Draw lines to indicate the glass panelling.

TELEPHONE   TELEPHONE

13

Big Ben

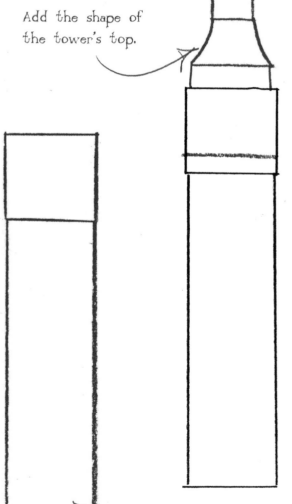

Big Ben is the name of the great bell in the Elizabeth Tower at the Palace of Westminster. However, the name is often used to refer to the tower as well.

Add the shape of the tower's top.

Add the steep pointed roof and the round clock face.

Draw four pinnacles on the top corners.

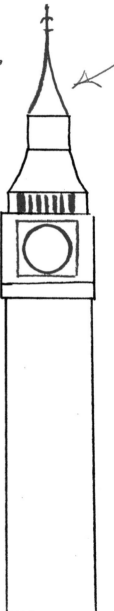

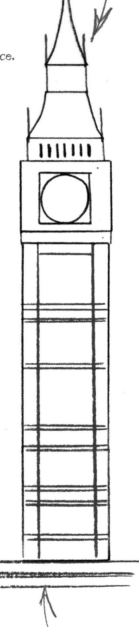

Sketch in the basic horizontal and vertical lines of the tower façade.

Begin by drawing a rectangle with a square on top.

Add detail to the roof and clock face. Draw vertical pillars on the sides of the tower.

Negative space

Negative space is the space around and between a picture's subject. Being aware of your drawing's negative space can help your compositions and is a good way to spot faults.

Use shading to give the tower a three-dimensional effect. Remember to shade areas where light would not reach.

Big Ben has interesting architectural details. The more you can add, the better your drawing will look.

Sketch in some background detail.

15

Black taxi cab

The black taxi is a symbol of metropolitan London. The test required to become a London taxi driver, 'The Knowledge', is considered the world's most difficult driver's exam.

When drawing complex objects it is sometimes easiest to begin by drawing a box in perspective.

Centreline

Now draw the main body of the taxi, using the centreline to help you get the details in the right places.

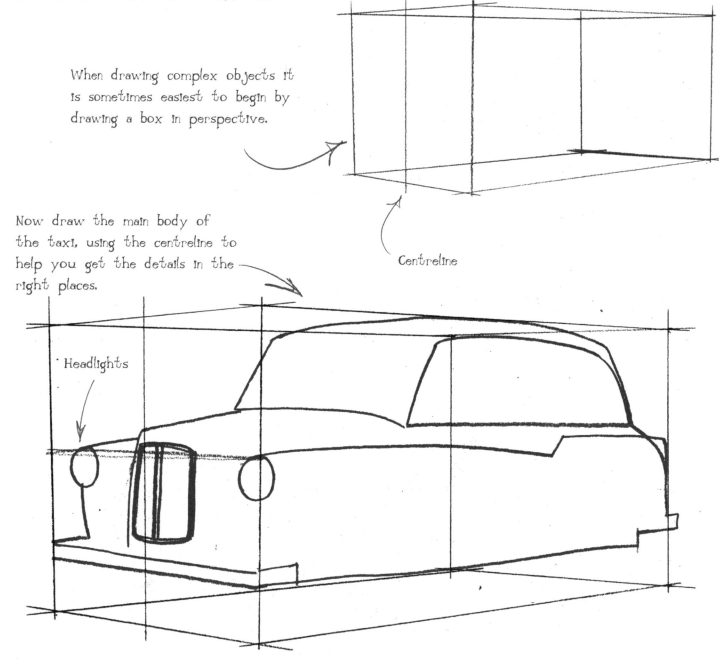

Headlights

Don't forget to add the distinctive taxi sign on the roof.

The car's wheel arch follows the direction of the perspective box. Indicate wheel rims with smaller ellipses.

Mark lines on the taxi for the doors and windows.

Add shading to the taxi. Leave some parts white as highlights.

Shade in the silhouette of the driver.

Remember to erase the construction lines of the box.

The position of the wipers can indicate the weather.

17

Buckingham Palace

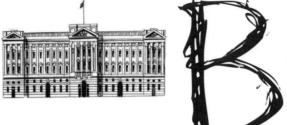

Buckingham Palace is the official London residence of the British monarch and the setting for many occasions of Royal hospitality.

The Union Flag is flown above the palace when the Queen is not in residence.

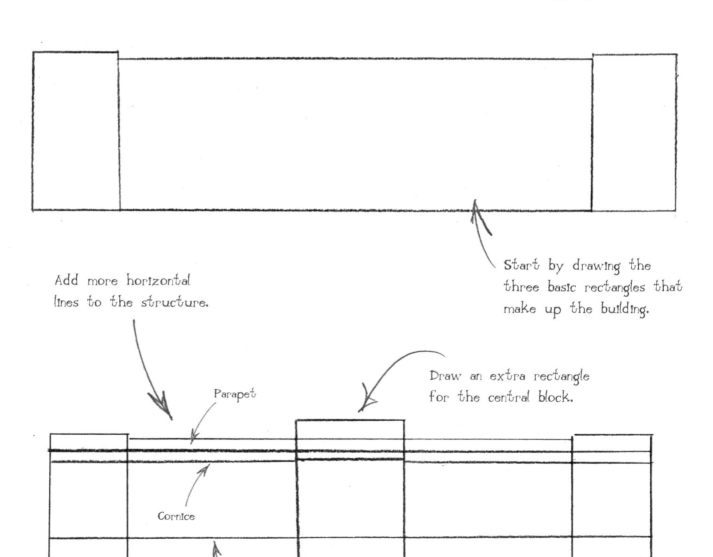

Start by drawing the three basic rectangles that make up the building.

Add more horizontal lines to the structure.

Draw an extra rectangle for the central block.

Parapet

Cornice

String course

Add three triangular pediments (gables).

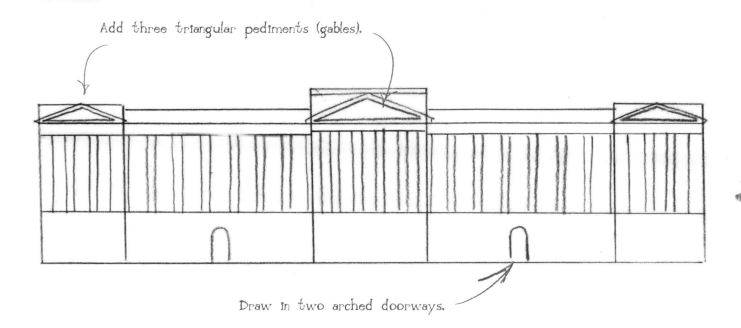

Draw in two arched doorways.

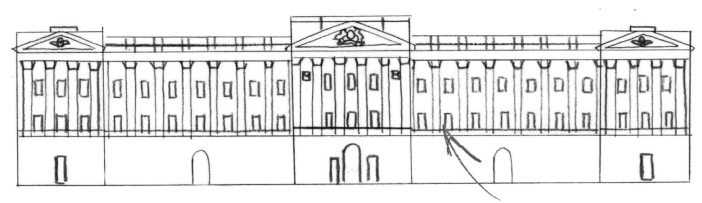

Draw in the rectangular windows and add capitals (tops) to the columns.

Shade the parts where light would not reach in order to show the palace's three dimensions.

Add the flag and flagpole.

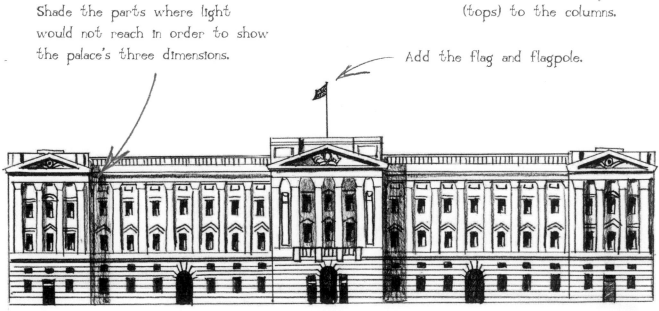

19

London bus

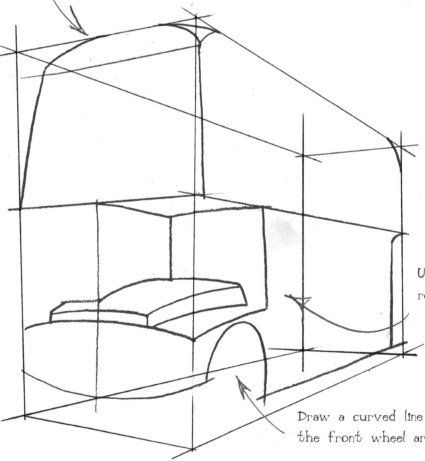

The Routemaster double-decker bus is recognised worldwide for its striking red livery and open rear platform.

Start by drawing a simple box in perspective.

Sketch the basic frame of the bus.

Using a centreline, sketch the recess next to the driver's cab.

Draw a curved line for the front wheel arch.

Add rectangular shapes for the windows on the top deck.

Using a mirror

Look at your drawing in a mirror. Seeing it in reverse is like looking at it through a fresh pair of eyes — it can help you to spot mistakes.

Draw the wheels with smaller ellipses for the rims.

Sketch headlights and the front detail of the bus.

Shade the interior of the bus as it would be seen from the outside.

Finish by adding the detail to the front of the bus. Choose your favourite place in London as the destination.

Add a shadow underneath the London bus and remove unwanted construction lines.

Add tone to the bus to give it a three-dimensional look.

21

Tower Bridge

Tower Bridge was designed to look like a fantasy castle to match the nearby Tower of London.

Start by drawing five rectangles to make the two towers and the connecting bridge.

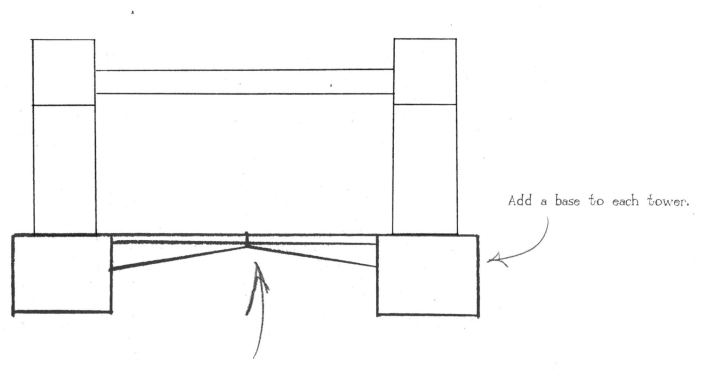

Add a base to each tower.

Draw in the rising section of the bridge using straight lines.

Add horizontal lines to mark the three storeys and draw the turrets of the towers.

Add a semicircle and a cross to show the way the cutwaters of the bridge project.

Draw in the windows and the walkway at the top.

Add the metal structure under the bridge.

Add tone to the towers so that they look like stone.

Finish by adding all remaining detail and a waterline.

Draw the side sections of the suspension bridge.

Scots Guardsman

The Foot Guards are famous for the Changing of the Guard ceremony. This man is a member of the Scots Guards; the buttons on his tunic are in groups of three.

Head

Shoulders

Hips

Draw three oval shapes for the head, shoulders and hips. Join with a line through the centre.

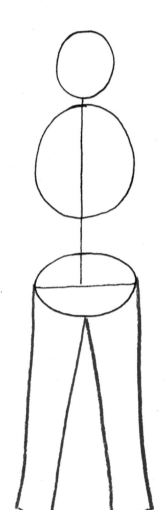

Give the guard legs and feet

Add an oval as the outline of the hat.

Sketch in arms and hand shapes.

Draw a jacket over the chest which is long enough to cover the hips.

Composition

By framing your drawing with a square or a rectangle, you can make it look completely different.

Draw a sentry box behind your guard using straight lines and a triangular roof.

Add tone to his uniform and texture to his bearskin hat.

Give the guard a rifle.

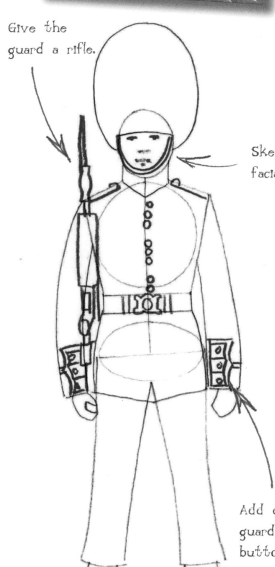

Sketch some facial features.

Shade the guard's trousers black and leave highlights on his shiny shoes.

Add detail to the guard's uniform, such as buttons and a belt.

25

Westminster Abbey

Westminster Abbey is the traditional location for the coronations of British monarchs; many are also buried there.

First, draw two tall rectangles.

Draw the outline of the Great West Door.

Define the sections of the tower.

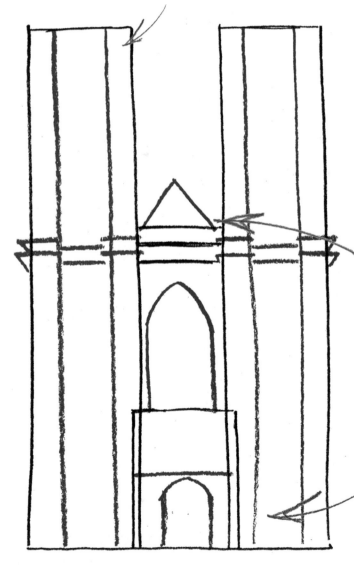

Sketch a triangle onto the middle section for a pointed roof.

Draw the main arch—shaped window and door.

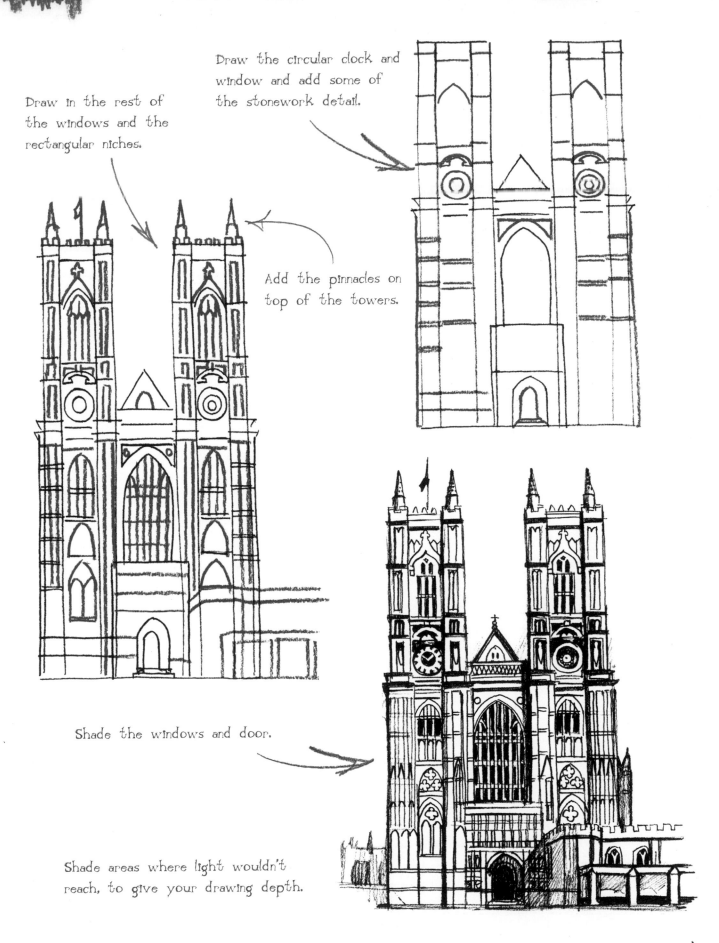

Draw the circular clock and window and add some of the stonework detail.

Draw in the rest of the windows and the rectangular niches.

Add the pinnacles on top of the towers.

Shade the windows and door.

Shade areas where light wouldn't reach, to give your drawing depth.

27

Yeoman of the Guard

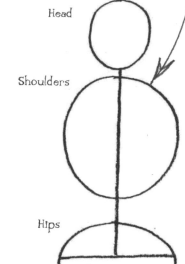

Start by drawing an upside-down T shape to mark the spine and hip line.

Head

Shoulders

Hips

Then add three oval shapes for the head, shoulders and hips.

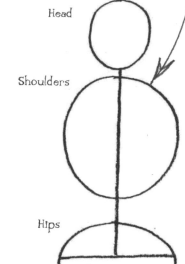

The Yeomen of the Guard are the Queen's ceremonial bodyguard. The Yeomen Warders of the Tower (known as 'Beefeaters') wear a very similar uniform.

Add the basic leg and foot shape.

Draw a circle at the ankles.

Draw the shape of the knee-length tunic using the spine line to mark the middle.

Outline the distinctive white ruff.

Add a belt between the chest and hips.

Sketch these simple shapes for the arms and hands.

Draw in the Tudor bonnet and sketch facial features.

Add details to the tunic.

Shade areas where light wouldn't reach.

Draw three lines to form the weapon in the guard's hand.

Complete the weapon.

Add detail to the knee breeches and stockings. Draw rosettes in the circles and define the heel of the shoes.

Finish the decorative detail on the guard's tunic. The traditional colours of the full dress uniform are scarlet and gold.

29

St Paul's Cathedral

St Paul's Cathedral has dominated the London skyline for 300 years, surviving the Blitz of the Second World War, to become one of the most important symbols of national identity.

Six rectangular blocks make up the base of the structure; draw a long centreline.

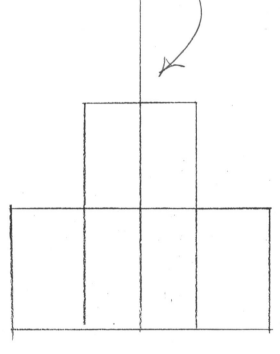

Use the centreline as a guide to draw the domed roof.

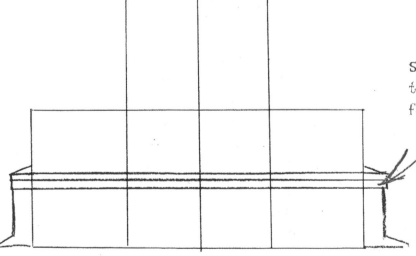

Sketch horizontal lines around the blocks you have drawn to form the ground-floor cornice.

Add straight lines to define the remaining levels and the towers.

Curved lines show the shape of the domed roof.

Draw in the windows.

Create the entrance by drawing a triangle on top of a rectangle.

Use shading to make the cathedral look three-dimensional.

Pairs of lines create the cathedral's many columns.

Complete your drawing by adding in the decorative details.

31

Glossary

Composition The arrangement of the parts of a picture on the drawing paper.

Construction lines Guidelines used in the early stages of a drawing; they may be erased later.

Fixative A type of resin sprayed over a drawing to prevent smudging. **It should only be used by an adult.**

Light source The direction from which the light seems to come in a drawing.

Negative space The empty space between the parts of a drawing, often an important part of the composition.

Perspective A method of drawing in which near objects are shown larger than faraway objects to give an impression of depth.

Proportion The correct relationship of scale between each part of the drawing.

Silhouette A drawing that shows only a flat dark shape, like a shadow.

Vanishing point (V.P.) The place in a perspective drawing where parallel lines appear to meet.

Index